CORE SKILLS

ANALYZE IT
LOOKING AT
TEXTS CRITICALLY

Gillian Gosman

PowerKiDS
press

New York

Published in 2015 by The Rosen Publishing Group, Inc.
29 East 21st Street, New York, NY 10010

First Edition

Editor: Caitie McAneney
Book Design: Mickey Harmon

Photo Credits: Cover (class) Tyler Olson/Shutterstock.com; cover (background) Attitude/Shutterstock.com; pp. 3–8, 10–12, 14–32 (dot backgrounds) vlastas/Shutterstock.com; pp. 5, 29 Monkey Business Images/Shutterstock.com; p. 6 BestPhotoStudio/Shutterstock.com; p. 7 monticello/Shutterstock.com; p. 9 (inset) llaszlo/Shutterstock.com; p. 9 (main) Hugh O'Connor/Shutterstock.com; p. 11 Jens Lennartsson/Getty Images; p. 13 kkaplin/Shutterstock.com; p. 14 Aromant/Shutterstock.com; p. 15 Jakub Zak/Shutterstock.com; p. 16 Don Nichols/Getty Images; p. 17 FloridaStock/Shutterstock.com; p. 18 Christine Langer-Pueschel/Shutterstock.com; p. 21 EVERT ELZINGA/AP Images; p. 22 sunabesyou/Shutterstock.com; p. 23 (columns) Panos Karas/Shutterstock.com; p. 23 (books) Africa Studio/Shutterstock.com; p. 25 Pressmaster/Shutterstock.com; p. 26 Levent Konuk/Shutterstock.com; p. 27 Valery Sidelnykov/Shutterstock.com; p. 30 Ditty_about_summer/Shutterstock.com.

Library of Congress Cataloging-in-Publication Data

Gosman, Gillian.
Analyze it: looking at texts critically / by Gillian Gosman.
p. cm. — (Core skills)
Includes index.
ISBN 978-1-4777-7386-4 (pbk.)
ISBN 978-1-4777-7387-1 (6-pack)
ISBN 978-1-4777-7385-7 (library binding)
1. Critical thinking — Juvenile literature. 2. Reading comprehension — Juvenile literature. 3. Problem solving — Juvenile literature. I. Gosman, Gillian. II. Title.
LB1590.3 G67 2015
370.15—d23

Manufactured in the United States of America

CPSIA Compliance Information: Batch #CW15PK: For Further Information contact Rosen Publishing, New York, New York at 1-800-237-9932

CONTENTS

TONS OF TEXT!

Students today are asked to read and understand many kinds of texts, from short stories and long novels to history textbooks and science laboratory reports. These texts can be separated into fiction, or literature, and nonfiction, or informational text.

Nonfiction texts are based on real people, events, and facts. Fiction texts describe imaginary people and events. Nonfiction texts cover different subjects, such as science and history. Fiction texts fall into many different genres, or kinds, which include fantasy, humor, and crime. Nonfiction and fiction texts are organized in specific ways and therefore present different challenges to readers.

In this book, we'll talk about skills for analyzing both literature and informational texts. Analyzing a text means studying it deeply, especially the structure and point of view.

QUICK TIP

Many times, readers only scan, or quickly read, a text for the information they need. Analyzing a text takes longer, but it helps you gain a better understanding of the text's meaning and purpose.

Analyzing a text helps you understand the author's purpose, *interpret* the meaning of the text, and form your own conclusions about it.

WHAT IS LITERATURE?

Literature is a genre that uses creative imagination, often in the form of a narrative. A narrative is a story. Short stories, myths, novels, poems, and plays are all considered literature. Novels are much longer than short stories. Plays are pieces of literature meant to be performed for an audience.

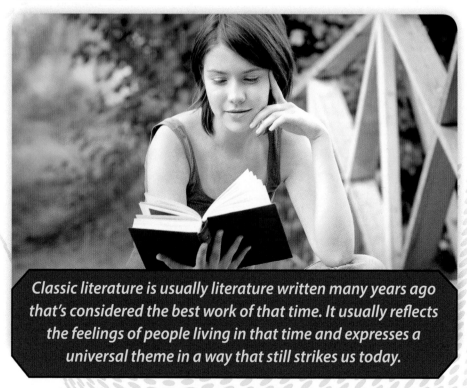

Classic literature is usually literature written many years ago that's considered the best work of that time. It usually reflects the feelings of people living in that time and expresses a universal theme in a way that still strikes us today.

Literature often expresses universal themes, such as love and hate. An author explores themes through their characters' **personalities** and actions. For example, a character might win the lottery and have to choose between using the money to save his poor family or buy himself a mansion. The character's decision shows readers the author's message about the struggle between kindness and personal greed.

QUICK TIP

How a character deals with a universal theme often shows the author's opinion of all people. Do people generally do the right thing, or are we easily tempted by personal greed? When looking for themes, ask yourself, "How does this character reflect qualities common to many people?" How can you relate to the character's struggle?

FICTION FEATURES

Many elements come together to make a work of literature. Literature introduces us to characters who experience events as the plot unfolds. The plot is the series of connected events that happen to the characters. One of these characters might be the narrator, or the voice telling us the story. This is often the main character, who is usually surrounded by secondary characters.

A story's plot is driven by conflict. Conflict is the struggle that takes place in the story. Some conflicts happen in a character's mind. These are called internal conflicts. Other conflicts occur between two characters, such as the main character and an evil **villain**.

QUICK TIP

Not all narrators are meant to be trusted! When we talk and write about narrators who present false or **biased** information, we refer to them as unreliable narrators.

A narrative takes place in one or more settings. Some stories take place in the city, while others take place in the wilderness. Each setting often has a particular mood, such as the comfort of home or the creepiness of a dark forest.

WHAT IS INFORMATIONAL TEXT?

Informational texts include nonfiction books, textbooks, brochures, and articles from newspapers and magazines. These texts are written with the purpose of informing readers about the world around them. Some scientific articles inform readers about new discoveries or experiments. Historical textbooks inform readers about a certain time period.

Informational texts often have special features to help readers understand the content. These features include visual illustrations, such as **diagrams** and photographs. Diagrams include charts, tables, and graphs. They illustrate data, or facts, to help readers understand their importance.

QUICK TIP

Informational texts generally have more text before and after the main body. Before the main body, you might find a table of contents, which is a list of chapter titles. At the end of a book, there may be a glossary, an index, and a bibliography, which is a list of sources used to write the text.

As you read, make notes in a notebook about the text. Include your questions, comments, and connections as you read.

The text might include vocabulary words, headings, sidebars, and discussion questions. Good readers often look over these additional features to get an idea of the topic and its key words, ideas, facts, and figures.

AUTHOR'S CLAIMS AND EVIDENCE

When the author of an informational text makes an argument that reflects their point of view, they're making a claim. Begin reading an informational text by identifying the author's claim. Generally, the claim appears in the introduction and is stated clearly.

Next, identify the author's reasons. Reasons are **concepts**, causes, or explanations that support the claim. Finally, check for evidence, or the facts and details that support the reasons. The strength of the argument depends on the strength of the evidence. Consider the source of the evidence. Does the author depend on firsthand evidence, such as data from a scientific experiment they performed on their own? Or does the author support their reasons with secondhand evidence, or work performed by someone else?

An example of a claim is "Climate change should be an important issue in this presidential election." The author would then give reasons why they believe this and support those reasons with data and other pieces of evidence.

CRAFT AND STRUCTURE

The author of a text spends a great deal of time crafting the structure of the work to make it as clear, interesting, and **logical** as possible. In literature, many texts are broken up into chapters or sections. Chapters are broken into paragraphs, and paragraphs are broken into sentences. The length of paragraphs and sentences says a lot about the author's writing style. The text is usually sprinkled with **dialogue** and creative description.

QUICK TIP

As you read a piece of literature, ask yourself why the author decided to break at a paragraph or chapter, or why they decided to include a description of something. For example, if the author spends a whole chapter describing a certain place or person, that place or person is probably very important to the main conflict or theme of the story.

Authors often have a certain style when it comes to the structure of their books. Some prefer to write short sentences and short chapters. Others prefer long sentences and chapters. Some prefer a lot of dialogue, while others prefer more description of the character's surroundings.

Many narratives are organized chronologically, or according to the order of events as they occurred. Sometimes, authors break chronological order to shift backward or forward in time. These breaks in the chronological structure are called flashbacks and flash-forwards. You can analyze an author's structure to understand the importance of plot points, new information, or a character's past.

The structure of an informational text can also tell you about an author's style and purpose. When reading informational texts, consider how the information is presented. Is the text structured chronologically? Does it use paragraphs to compare and contrast two or more things? Maybe it explains how a cause led to an effect. It could also identify a problem and suggest a solution.

An author of a scientific paper on climate change might structure their argument as cause and effect. They might argue that as gas and oil use increase, severe weather events also increase.

An author might argue that as global temperatures increase, major ice sheets are disappearing, which has a negative effect on polar bear populations. This is another example of a cause-and-effect argument.

The author of an informational text may include just the plain facts, or they might include interviews, short personal stories, and even humor. If they're writing for an older, professional audience, they might write a block of text with difficult language. However, if they're writing for a younger audience or students, they might include diagrams, headings, and simple language.

POINT OF VIEW

A point of view is an individual's position on a topic. For example, does an author agree or disagree that bullying is a major issue? Does a character believe in true love? An individual's point of view is often determined by their age, gender, location, education, social class, and past experience.

The point of view of an informational text refers to the author's position. Point of view occurs in persuasive texts. An author's point of view can be biased, which makes the information unreliable. A critical reader is always on the lookout for biased information.

QUICK TIP

To tell if an author is biased, ask yourself these questions. Does their evidence seem reliable or questionable? Do they seem to be trying to sway the reader's emotions? Check other sources on the same topic to compare evidence and points of view, and decide which seems more reliable.

Each character in literature has a point of view. It shapes the way they experience and respond to the events in the plot and how they act with others. This is one way you can compare characters in a book. Ask yourself, what does this character believe in?

When we talk about the narrator's point of view in a piece of literature, we're talking about where they fit in the story. There are three common points of view:

First person
The narrator is a central character in the plot. This point of view uses "I" and "we."
Example: "I went on an adventure today."

Second person
The narrator is speaking to the reader as if the reader is in the story. This point of view uses "you." This is rarely used.
Example: "You went on an adventure today."

Third person
The narrator is observing the action from the outside. This point of view uses "he," "she," and "they."
Example: "They went on an adventure today."

THE CONTEXT

A text is created at a specific time, in a specific place, and in a specific society. These **contexts** shape many features of the texts, such as its genre, its subject matter and themes, its point of view, and its audience.

When reading literature, keep in mind that the author and the characters are shaped by their contexts. A character may have certain beliefs, values, and even biases that are unfamiliar to modern readers. Their knowledge and understanding of the world may be different from our own.

Context is important when reading informational texts, too. Be sure to note the date and place the text was published. As you read, ask yourself if the information is still considered correct. Have new understandings or new information made the text out of date or incorrect?

It's good to research, or study, the context of a book before you read it or as you read it. For example, if you were to read *The Diary of Anne Frank*, you might research World War II and the Holocaust. This will help you understand why Anne Frank wrote her diary and why it was important in that time and place.

DOES THE TEXT MAKE SENSE?

Whether you're reading literature or informational texts, you'll probably come across words and concepts you don't know. Luckily, there are a few ways of understanding the meaning of unfamiliar terms. If you have access to reference materials, such as a dictionary, they can provide definitions. Informational texts such as this book often contain bolded vocabulary words, which are defined within the body of the text, in a sidebar, or in a glossary.

QUICK TIP

You can make an educated guess at the meaning of an unfamiliar word by looking at its root. For example, the root "bio" is from the ancient Greek word for "life." Words that include the root "bio," such as "biology," have to do with life.

What if you don't have reference materials to depend on? The text itself can be your guide! You can use context clues, which are the words, illustrations, and headings surrounding the unfamiliar word or concept. How does the unfamiliar word fit into its sentence or paragraph? Is it compared or contrasted to another word?

Get to know your word roots. Here's a list of common Greek and Latin roots. Once you learn them, you'll see them everywhere you go!

root word	meaning	example
chron	time	chronology
fort	strong	fortress
geo	earth	geography
graph	write	autograph
hydr	water	hydrant
phone	sound	homophone
tele	distant	telephone
zo	animal	zoology

WHERE DOES IT FIT?

No text stands alone. All texts are part of a larger conversation about a particular topic or theme. As you read, try to **integrate** new information with what you've already read and evaluate the author's contribution to the conversation. Where does the text fit in the conversation?

Begin by thinking about what you already know about a topic. Then, consider what new information, point of view, structure, and vocabulary a new text offers. When reading literature, ask yourself how the author contributes to the already existing literature on a particular theme. For example, if you're reading a story about slavery, how does it stand apart and add to other literature about slavery? When reading an informational text, ask yourself how the author adds new information or presents it in a new way.

Imagine you have to write a report on a book about pilots in World War I. You might want to check out other books on World War I—both literature and informational text—to see how your book relates to other books on the topic.

QUICK TIP

Don't limit yourself to books! Does a novel remind you of a song you've heard? Does an idea discussed in your social studies book remind you of a movie you've seen? Making these kinds of connections will add to your understanding of both texts.

COMPARING TEXTS

Comparing texts is a good way to analyze an author's purpose and perspective. When you're comparing two pieces of literature, you can look at the similarities and differences between many fiction features, including character, setting, and point of view. One story about the American civil rights movement might be set in a school, while another might be set in a factory. What does that say about each story and what the authors are trying to say?

QUICK TIP

It's important to use critical thinking while comparing informational texts. Critical thinking means not just accepting what an author says, but analyzing and evaluating it, then deciding whether or not you accept the author's claims. Ask yourself if one text seems more biased than another or if one has better evidence than another.

Comparing informational texts is very important because you need to study multiple sides of an argument to get closer to the "truth." Two or more professionals in the field may disagree about an important idea. Two firsthand accounts of an event might be different. Consider how differences might reflect the various points of view at play.

FORMING YOUR OWN OPINION

You've read a text, evaluated how it fits into a larger conversation, and compared it with similar texts. Now, it's time to form your own opinion. When speaking or writing about any kind of text, it's important to support your claims with clear reasons, which are supported by strong evidence.

Imagine you're writing an essay about the fairy tale *Cinderella*. You've decided that kindness is an important theme of the story. After stating your claim, you must present your reasons—at least three—for believing this. Your first reason might be that Cinderella is kind to her stepmother and stepsisters. Next, you must provide evidence of this kindness, using specific details and, if possible, quotations from the story.

QUICK TIP

A quotation is an excellent form of evidence. Just as important as the quotation is the credit you give to the original author. This credit is called a citation. Ask your teacher which citation format they prefer.

An outline can be a great tool for writing your essay. It can be hard to keep track of claims, reasons, and pieces of evidence, so write it all down and organize your thoughts before you begin your essay. Be sure your three reasons are clearly different from one another. Be sure each piece of evidence directly proves the reason it supports.

YOU'RE READY TO READ!

It takes a lot of effort to analyze a text! You must be familiar with its genre and the common features of that kind of text. You must determine the point of view, the meanings of unfamiliar words, the structure of the text, and the context of its publication. You must integrate new information with what you already know and evaluate the author's themes or arguments based on the evidence given and your own experience. Finally, you must be prepared to speak and write about your analysis, stating claims and supporting them with reasons and evidence.

Mastering these skills will take time and effort. It'll also take a lot of research and reading. However, taking time to analyze will give you insight into the true message of a text!

GLOSSARY

biased (BY-uhsd) Showing a personal preference for or dislike of something or someone.

concept (KAHN-sehpt) An idea.

context (KAHN-tehkst) The circumstances around something.

diagram (DY-uh-gram) A drawing that shows how elements are arranged or related.

dialogue (DY-uh-lahg) Part of a written work with two or more characters speaking.

evaluate (ih-VAL-yuh-wayt) To weigh the importance or truth of something.

integrate (IHN-tuh-grayt) To bring different parts together to form a whole.

interpret (ihn-TUHR-pruht) To explain the meaning of something.

logical (LAH-jih-kuhl) Well thought out and reasonable.

minority (muh-NOHR-uh-tee) A part of a population that is in some way different from the larger part of a population.

personality (puhr-suh-NAA-luh-tee) The qualities that mark an individual.

villain (VIH-luhn) A wicked or evil person.

INDEX

WEBSITES

Due to the changing nature of Internet links, PowerKids Press has developed an online list of websites related to the subject of this book. This site is updated regularly. Please use this link to access the list: www.powerkidslinks.com/cosk/ana